PAYING YOUR BILLS

AND GETTING

MEDICAL TREATMENT

HOW MAINTENANCE AND CURE LAWS
PROTECT YOU AFTER A MARITIME INJURY

TIMOTHY YOUNG

THE YOUNG FIRM
WWW.JONESACTLAW.COM

Table of Contents

Table of Contents

PART 1: THE BASICS

What is the Jury Told When They Consider My Maintenance and Cure Claim?

OK, let's cut right to the important stuff. What laws are actually told to the jury when they are considering your maintenance and cure rights? What law does the jury apply to your maintenance and cure claims? Well, here are the ACTUAL jury instructions that the United States Fifth Circuit Court of Appeal says should be read to the jury regarding maintenance and cure. This federal Fifth Circuit court overseas the states of Louisiana, Mississippi, Texas and others. IMPORTANT NOTE—In 2009, the law regarding punitive damages for failing to pay a maintenance and cure claim changed. A seaman can now seek punitive damages in addition to the other damages listed in the attached jury charges. The law on maintenance and cure got better for injured maritime workers in 2009! The attached charges are from 2006 and the Fifth Circuit has not revised them to reflect this change in the law, BUT courts still apply the new law in addition to the attached charges.

What Damages Can I Get If My Company Refuses To Pay Maintenance And Cure?

If your company refuses to pay maintenance and cure and it is later determined that your maintenance and cure was wrongfully denied, there are three separate levels of damages which you can obtain. The types of damages depend upon the level of fault against your company in regards to its refusal to pay maintenance and cure benefits.

Under the first level, if your company just wrongfully denies maintenance and cure benefits to you, you can obtain attorney fees associated with having to file suit and obtain a judgment in order to get your maintenance and cure benefits. The law allows for attorney fees to be collected by you in regard to your maintenance and cure claim if it is determined that your maintenance and cure was "wrongfully" denied.

Under the next level of damages, if it is not only determined that your company wrongfully denied you maintenance and cure but it is also determined that your company arbitrarily and unreasonably denied you maintenance and cure, you can then collect additional damages for any worsening of your medical condition. This means that if you suffered more pain or if your injury got worse because you were denied medical treatment, not only can you collect your medical payments which you should have been paid, but you can also collect additional damages from your company.

Finally, under the third and most important level, if it is determined that your company intentionally wrongfully denied you maintenance and cure, and arbitrarily did so, you can collect punitive damages against your company for failing to pay maintenance and cure benefits. This law was recently revised and the United States Supreme

Court clearly declared that punitive damages were available for maintenance and cure claims if it can be shown that your company acted intentionally and arbitrarily. We applaud this Supreme Court decision of Townsend v. Atlantic Sounding which finally declares clearly that punitive damages are available when you pursue your maintenance and cure claim against your company. This law has made it much easier for our office to obtain much needed medical treatment and maintenance benefits for our injured maritime Jones Act clients.

What Is A Declaratory Judgment Lawsuit Against Me In Regards To My Maintenance And Cure Rights?

Often employers will actually file a claim against an injured employee in federal court under what is known as a declaratory judgment action. The purpose of this claim is to have the federal court declare that you have reached maximum cure and that your employer no longer owes you maintenance and cure. This is a preemptive-type suit wherein your company takes the offensive and actually goes to court to have your maintenance and cure rights declared terminated. Generally your company is not seeking any type of money or damages from you, but rather it is simply seeking a legal opinion from a judge that you have reached maximum cure or maximum improvement and that your company no longer owes you maintenance and cure.

Ironically, you are entitled to file a counterclaim under the Jones Act against your employer arising out of such declaratory actions. In other words, if your company files a declaratory action against you relating to your maintenance and cure, you can not only answer the lawsuit, but you can also file your own claim directly against your employer.

Our office has been very successful in obtaining significant judgments and settlements for our clients when we have actually filed their claims within the declaratory judgment action. Even though your company is asking the court to rule in their favor, you are entitled to have the court consider your claims including potential Jones Act claims for negligence. In this way, not only can the judge deny your company's claim against you, but he can actually rule in your favor and award you money damages under the Jones Act.

Also, if you file a Jones Act claim within the declaratory judgment action, you are then entitled to present all claims to a jury rather than a judge. In doing so, a jury will decide whether you have reached maximum improvement or maximum cure under your maintenance and cure claim. The jury would also be allowed to decide the merits of your Jones Act negligence claim against your company.

We usually recommend that this approach is taken since it takes your maintenance and sure claim away from the judge and allows a jury to decide your rights. Generally, a company is more comfortable having a judge decide your case rather than an unknown jury; although this will vary depending upon the judge assigned to your case.

Will My Maintenance And Cure Be Stopped If I Get Released By The Doctor?

Generally, under maintenance and cure law your employer only has to pay you maintenance and cure until you reach maximum cure or maximum medical improvement This typically occurs once your treating doctor releases you from his care. In other words, it is very likely that your rights to maintenance and cure will stop once you are released by your treating physician. This is one reason it is critical that you choose a physician that you know and trust for your medical treatment. Very often company-chosen physicians will prematurely release you and declare that you are at maximum improvement even though they have not performed basic medical testing to determine the nature and extent of any possible injuries.

What Is The Standard I Must Prove In Order To Win My Maintenance And Cure Claim?

Under the landmark decision of Vaughan v. Atkinson, the United States Supreme Court held that all doubts and ambiguities are to be resolved in favor of the seaman in regard to maintenance and cure claim. This means that there is a very light burden of proof for you to win your maintenance and cure claim.

This favorable case law can be very helpful in demanding that your employer pay maintenance and cure as your case progresses. All employers understand that a jury will be told that all doubts and ambiguities are to be resolved in your favor at trial. Although this does still require that you present sufficient proof to win your claim, you have less of a burden to win your maintenance and cure case than does your employer. The law favors awarding maintenance and cure rather than denying it to you.

Do I Get A Jury Trial Or A Judge Trial For My Maintenance And Cure Claim?

Maintenance and cure claims fall under general maritime law. Under general maritime law, neither party has the right to a trial by jury. However, the answer does not end there.

If you join your maritime claim for maintenance and cure with another basis for a jury trial, very often you can obtain the right to a jury trial in regard to your maintenance and cure claim. For example, if you also file a Jones Act claim under the federal statute known as the Jones Act, you do have the right to a jury trial in regard to your Jones Act claim. Courts have ruled that as long as your maritime law maintenance and cure claim is joined with and filed with a Jones Act claim you also obtain the right to a jury in regard to your maritime maintenance and cure claim. In such situations a jury will hear both cases and decide both cases at the same time.

However, if for some reason you cannot successfully pursue a Jones Act claim and your only rights fall under maritime law against your employer, then you will not have the right to a jury trial in regard to your maintenance and cure claim. Examples could be if an individual is on shore leave and becomes injured through no fault of his employer. Under such circumstances, his injury may technically fall under maintenance and cure law, but because his employer played no role whatsoever in causing his injury, there would not be a valid Jones Act claim to pursue along with the maintenance and cure claim, leaving only a non-jury maritime law claim.

It should be remembered that often a trial by judge is preferred to a jury trial. This is especially true in regard to a maintenance and cure claim without a Jones Act claim. In such situations many judges understand that all doubt and ambiguities are to be resolved in favor of the seaman in regard to the maintenance and cure claim. It is often possible to receive a more favorable ruling from a judge in regard to a maintenance and cure claim than you may receive from a jury. It simply depends upon the facts of your case and the judge assigned to your case.

Where Can I File My Maintenance And Cure Case?

Many of our clients ask in which courthouse they can file their maintenance and cure claim. Generally maintenance and cure claims can be filed in multiple locations. If you worked for a company and traveled out of southeast Louisiana, chances are very good that you can actually file your claim in southeast Louisiana even if your company is based out of Texas or another state. This is true even if you live in Mississippi, Alabama, or a state other than Louisiana. The fact that you traveled in and out of southeast Louisiana to work for your company may mean that your case can be filed in southeast Louisiana.

Additionally, where you received much of your medical treatment may also serve as a proper location to file your suit. But this depends on whether or not your company itself can be sued in the state in which you received your medical treatment. For example, many Louisiana companies and Texas companies do not officially do business in the states of Mississippi, Alabama, or other Gulf South states other than Texas and Louisiana.

In short, generally there is more than one location where you can choose to file your maintenance and cure claim. If your company does business out of Louisiana and/or you received significant medical treatment in Louisiana and your company conducts any business at all in Louisiana, in all likelihood you can file your maintenance and cure claim in the State of Louisiana.

How Long Do I Get Maintenance And Cure?

Maintenance and cure are due to an injured seaman until the seaman reaches 'maximum cure' in regards to the injury or illness which occurred while in the service of the vessel. This term is a medical term which generally refers to when the injured seaman's medical condition will not get any better. Although the condition may require pain management or pain treatment, and the condition may be seriously disabling to the injured seaman including permanent restrictions, once the seaman is released by his physician, his rights to maintenance and cure generally end. Again, the legal test is when a medical expert concludes that the seaman has

14

reached maximum cure, or maximum improvement, in regard to his injury or illness.

However, it is critical to note that often medical experts disagree in regard to maximum cure. Many times one doctor will recommend further treatment including potential surgery when another doctor believes that the injured seaman can return to work, even full-duty work. This is very common when a company-chosen doctor disagrees with a more neutral doctor chosen by the seaman and unaffiliated with the company. In these common situations, it is often necessary to present the issue whether an injured seaman has reached maximum cure to a judge or jury for determination. In such cases the injured seaman is allowed to present his claim for maintenance and cure to a jury if the seaman is also pursuing a claim under the Jones Act against his employer.

PART 2: CURE ISSUES

What Is Cure?

The term cure refers to any and all (1) curative medical expenses which (2) are reasonably necessary and (3) arise out of an illness or injury that you have (4) while in the service of the vessel. There are four points to this definition of cure.

First, cure generally entails only curative treatment, and not palliative treatment. This means that your employer must pay only for medical treatment which is resulting or could result in a betterment of your condition. If the treatment simply relieves pain, generally it is not included under cure expenses. (However, it is critical to remember that pain-relieving treatment is included under any type of Jones Act claim that you may pursue.)

Next, the medical expenses must be reasonable and necessary. This is one of the main reasons why we urge injured seamen to avoid long treatment from company-chosen physicians. Once a company-chosen physician discharges you as having reached maximum cure, it is often impossible to get your employer to re-start payment of cure for you. It is critical that you understand that your cure rights legally end when it is determined that you have reached 'maximum cure'. This determination can be made by any qualified physician. Often physicians disagree as to whether an injured seaman has reached maximum cure. Unfortunately, if your employer obtains a medical opinion from their chosen physician stating that you have reached maximum cure, most employers will immediately terminate maintenance and cure benefits. This includes your critical medical payments which your employer was legally responsible to pay for you. We always recommend that our clients choose their own treating physician to avoid having a premature and/or unreliable opinion that they have reached maximum cure.

The definition above is also limited to any 'illness or injury'. The illness or injury part of this definition simply means that you have suffered some type of illness *or* injury while in the service of the vessel. Not only does this include typical accident related injuries such as neck, back, knee and other physical injuries, but cure also includes any reasonable and necessary medical expenses relating to illnesses which are suffered while in the service of the vessel. Our office has handled many cases involving stroke victims, as well as infectious diseases which occurred while our client was in the service of the vessel. These illnesses were not actually caused by the vessel work, but simply manifested while our client was working. Still, in such cases they are generally included under maintenance and cure.

Finally, the above definition of cure states that the illness or injury must occur while you are in the service of the vessel. Fortunately, for seamen, this does *not* mean that the illness or injury must actually occur while you are *on* the vessel. Many workers work overseas and during the course of their regular employment travel to and from the vessel. Additionally, many employees are given shore leave even while they are still working aboard the vessel. Your illness or injury does not have to actually occur on the vessel for it to be included under maritime law of maintenance and cure. The term 'service of the vessel' is very broad and often extends beyond and off of the vessel.

What Does Medicaid Have To Do With My Maintenance and Cure Rights?

Under maintenance and cure law, your employer must pay all of your reasonable and necessary medical expenses from a physician that you choose. However, there is an unfortunate twist in the law which states that if you are able to obtain medical treatment from a public facility, or from a public social program such as Medicaid/Medicare, then your company is not obligated to pay for such medical costs. This essentially allows your company to dump its responsibility for your medical treatment off to social programs such as Medicaid or Medicare.

One of the truly horrible effects of this loophole is that many companies will initially deny medical benefits to an injured seaman. In turn, this seaman is then forced to apply for Medicaid and seek medical treatment through public social service programs. Once the seaman then qualifies for Medicaid, the employer uses this as a further excuse to continue to deny medical treatment to the injured seaman. It becomes a circle that the injured seaman cannot get out of.

Our office has handled many situations where an employer has tried to force a seaman to obtain

Medicaid. We always send strong demand letters to companies demanding that they pay for our client's cure benefits. It is very important that the company be placed on written notice to pay for all current and ongoing medical expenses. It is also important to bring the company to court as quickly as possible so that the injured seaman does not have to ultimately apply for and rely on public social service programs such as Medicaid or Medicare. As we all know, much of the medical treatment provided by these programs is not the same type of treatment that you can obtain from a highly paid private physician who is an expert in his field. Unfortunately, many physicians do not accept Medicaid or Medicare and an injured seaman is then left with fewer choices of physicians if he must rely upon such a program.

What Is Palliative Versus Curative Treatment?

Under cure law, you are only entitled to receive medical treatment that is curative in nature. This is in contrast to medical treatment which is considered to be palliative in nature.

One easy way to think of the difference between palliative and curative is will the medical treatment result in a betterment of your condition. In other words, medical treatment which is "curative" is treatment which is actually getting you better. Palliative treatment, on the other hand, is treatment which simply relieves pain. As crazy as it sounds, under maintenance and cure law your employer is not obligated to pay for medical treatment which simply relieves pain and does not result in a betterment or improvement of your condition. This can include many types of medical treatment including management as well as pain medications which many people stay on for years following a serious injury. Unfortunately, under maintenance and cure laws, your employer can likely argue that it is not responsible for payment of pain medication.

Even though palliative treatment is not covered under maintenance and cure law, remember that you can obtain pain management treatment as well as any other type of palliative treatment under the Jones Act if you are successful with a Jones Act claim. This is one major reason that you should always file a Jones Act claim with your general Maritime Law maintenance and cure claim. Many medical expenses which may not be covered under maintenance and cure laws are covered under the Jones Act.

Do I Get My Choice Of Doctor To Provide Cure Treatment For Me?

Yes, under maritime law you are entitled to select your own choice of treating physician. Unfortunately, this does not always play out in a clean, clear way with your company. Often your company will insist that you begin initial medical treatment with its company-chosen physician.

Then, once that company-chosen physician quickly issues a discharge release to you and states that you have reached maximum cure, your employer will then refuse to authorize and approve treatment from a physician that you seek to choose at that time. In other words, many employers will use an unreliable and premature release from a company-chosen physician to refuse to authorize and approve further treatment from a physician that you choose. In these situations our office immediately steps in and pays for independent medical treatment for our clients so that we can prove the full nature and extent of their illnesses and injuries.

Remember, it is your right under maritime law to select your own treating physician. If your employer gives you any option to do so, you should always select your own physician to provide treatment after your maritime injury or illness.

You should also insist that your company approve a doctor you select. If your company will not do so at the outset of your injury, most likely it will treat you even worse as your claim progresses.

Should I Go To A Company-Chosen Doctor For My Cure Treatment?

The short answer is absolutely not. You are only entitled to cure until a qualified physician determines that you have reached "maximum cure".

We have seen many cases when a company-chosen physician provides initial treatment and within weeks or months determines that the employee has reached maximum cure. This same individual may still be experiencing severe pain and physical problems but because the company-chosen physician has discharged the employee, his rights to maintenance and cure are then terminated by his company.

We urge all of our clients to select their own choice of physician for treatment. Although your company is entitled to investigate your claim for maintenance and cure which does include sending you to its choice of physician, generally they are only allowed to have their physician examine you on one occasion to provide his opinion in court if necessary. This does not include ongoing treatment which is one of the most common mistakes injured seamen make after a work accident.

Your rights to cure, including all reasonable and necessary medical expenses that you may need in regards to your illness or injury, hinges on whether or not you have been discharged by a qualified physician as having reached maximum cure.

Every time you continue ongoing treatment with a company-chosen physician you are risking that he will unreasonably and prematurely discharge you before the full extent of your injury has been determined. This is especially true since many company-chosen physicians hesitate to perform basic testing which can identify serious illnesses or injuries.

Countless times we have seen our clients discharged by the company physician after only weeks of treatment without even having an MRI performed.

When we become involved in their cases, we immediately obtain basic medical testing including MRIs. Often these MRIs show serious lumbar and cervical problems including herniated discs.

PART 3: MAINTENANCE ISSUES

Why Is It Better To Receive Maintenance Rather Than Advances?

There are several reasons why it is better to receive the highest rate of maintenance possible rather than allowing your employer to simply categorize the payments to you as advances. As we all know, injured seamen will typically receive maintenance payments but most employers will also pay an additional payment as advances each month. This has several unfortunate effects to the injured seaman.

First, many advances are categorized as wages by your employer. This means that your employer is essentially continuing to pay you wages while you are injured after your maritime accident. Unfortunately, this also means that these payments are taxable to you the same as wages would be if you had continued to work. Maintenance payments, however, are generally not taxable income to you. This means that the more money you can have classified as maintenance by your employer, the less tax you will owe at the end of the year.

Additionally, advances are often viewed as amounts that the injured employee must pay back at the end of any type of claim or settlement. In reality, this very rarely happens but if your case does go to court, your employer will absolutely try to take credit for the advances that your employer previously provided to you. In every case in which our clients receive advances that is ultimately tried to a judge or a jury, each employer will proudly declare to the jury that it voluntarily provided advances to our client which it did not legally have to do under the law. We strongly disagree with this statement and we often argue to the jury that our client was entitled to the money anyway as maintenance payments. Unfortunately, the employers often gain points with the judge or jury by trying to say that they paid the injured maritime worker more than they had to under the law. By making sure that your company pays the highest rate of maintenance possible, you can avoid any arguments that your company was voluntarily paying additional payments to you.

Are Your Maintenance Payments Taxable Income?

Generally, maintenance payments are considered the same as state workers' compensation payments for purposes of income taxes. This means that usually you do not have to pay federal income tax on any maintenance payments that you receive during your maritime injury. However, it is important to check your own state law to determine whether or not you have to pay state income tax on maintenance payments which you may receive from your employer after a maritime injury.

Also, it is very important to note the difference between maintenance payments and advances. Many advances are actually paid as "wages" by your maritime employer after your injury. In other words, many employers will simply continue to pay wages to you following your injury even though your employer should legally be categorizing such payments as maintenance. This has the unfortunate effect of requiring you to pay taxes on such advances, the same as you would if you were receiving regular wages. So, while maintenance payments may not be taxable to you, there is a very good likelihood that advances will be taxable to you especially if they are classified by your employer as wages to you.

If I Live Rent Free With A Family Member, Does My Company Still Have To Pay Maintenance To Me?

Unfortunately, there is what we consider a loophole in the maintenance and cure law which states that a company does not have to pay maintenance benefits to an injured seaman if he is able to live rent free with either a family member or other individual. We see this all the time with many of our much younger clients, some of whom still live at home with their parents while they work offshore or on vessels. When this individual becomes injured, he simply returns home and lives rent free as he was prior to his accident. This generally occurs with very young individuals in their late teens or early 20s. As horrible as it seems, the company then uses this as an excuse to deny maintenance benefits to this individual.

Another situation we see often is when an individual and his family actually have rent bills and monthly expenses but because his company is denying maintenance benefits to him, he is forced to change his living arrangements and move back in with family members or relatives. In this situation, the company later denies maintenance benefits to this individual because he is now living "rent free". It infuriates us that the company has forced this individual and often his family to return home or to move in with other family members or relatives since the company was refusing to pay maintenance benefits.

There are many tricky loopholes in maintenance and cure laws, and it is important that you handle your case properly. Call us if you have any questions whatsoever about whether the steps that you are considering may ultimately hurt your maintenance and cure case. We want you to understand your rights, choices, and options, and we want to make sure you do not unknowingly hurt your maintenance and cure claim.

What Are Advances Which I Receive With My Monthly Maintenance Check?

Many of our clients receive "advances" in addition to "maintenance" payments each month. The term "advances" is used by companies to describe what *they* believe are additional payments above and beyond what *they* believe to be your proper rate of maintenance. Notice that I said what '*they*' believe to be your proper rate of maintenance. It has been our experience that almost all companies pay a grossly low rate of maintenance of approximately $15.00 to $40.00 per day. Then, these same companies will pay additional "advances" so that you can afford to actually pay your monthly bills. Whenever our office becomes involved in a maritime Jones Act injury case, we immediately notify the company that our client requires the full payments each month in order to pay his monthly bills. We do not care if the company characterizes the extra payments as "advances" or labels the payments under maintenance. The point is that every maritime company should pay the full amount that an injured seaman needs to pay his monthly bills as the maintenance payment each month. The term "advances" is simply the way most companies try to characterize, or more accurately mis-characterize, what they believe to be additional payments above and beyond maintenance. We strongly recommend that you send your company a detailed listing of your monthly bills at the outset of your claim so that your company is then on notice concerning how much it actually takes for you to pay your monthly bills.

One final thought about advances. Many of our clients actually have short-term disability and long-term disability policies through their company. We *immediately* advise these clients to apply for short-term disability and long-term disability following their injuries. Then, if their company ever attempt to reduce or terminate what they characterize as advances, our clients can seek full payment through their disability insurance policies.

Call our office to discuss how you can avoid having your advances terminated and the other sources you can pursue to help pay your monthly bills.

Can I Collect Disability While I Am Receiving Maintenance Payments?

Many of our clients ask if they are entitled to file for and collect short-term disability or long-term disability payments even while they are also receiving maintenance payments. The answer is yes, individuals can apply for and receive short-term and long-term disability even though you are also receiving maintenance payments. We actually encourage most workers to be sure to file for disability under their STD/LTD policies. However, most disability insurance policies do take a "credit" for any maintenance payments being paid to you. This means your disability payments will likely be reduced by the amount of maintenance that you are receiving at that time. But because disability payments are usually much higher than your maintenance payments, you still end up getting additional money from your disability policy.

It is very important to understand that your short-term disability and long-term disability insurance policies are very separate from any rights that you have under maritime law in regard to maintenance and cure. This is also true in regard to any potential Jones Act claim which you may have after your accident and injury. Your short-term disability and long-term disability policies are issued by a company separate from your company. When you file a claim against your short-term disability and long-term disability policies, you are filing an entirely separate claim against a third-party insurance company. This claim actually has nothing to do with any claims that you may have against your company for maintenance and cure and/or under the Jones Act. Although some large employers will administer the short-term disability payments, it is still a separate claim and you should always pursue and file disability claims even if you are receiving maintenance payments.

Call us immediately if you have any questions about your maintenance payments and the other avenues that may be available to you outside of maintenance and cure laws. Be sure to order our maritime injury law tool kit which will educate you about your rights, choices and options. The tool kit is absolutely free and we will ship it to you immediately so that you can learn your rights in the privacy of your home.

What Should Be Included In My Monthly Maintenance Amount?

Maintenance is defined as the amount of money it takes for the injured seaman to pay his monthly bills while he is injured and until he reaches maximum cure from an injury or illness which occurred while in the service of the vessel. There are numerous cases which debate the actual items which should be included in calculating the injured seaman's "monthly expenses". At a minimum, these expenses include the cost of food, lodging, and electricity. Often the seaman can also collect maintenance for bills such as insurance payments, vehicle payments, heating oil, phone bills, and other typical monthly bills.

We strongly suggest that any injured seaman immediately send his employer a detailed list of his monthly bills after he suffers an injury or illness. By providing your employer with a monthly expense form it makes it difficult for your employer to later argue that they did not know how much your monthly expenses were at the time of your injury. This builds the record on the amount of maintenance that you might require month to month. Even though your employer may refuse to pay such maintenance, at least it is clear on the record that your employer is refusing to pay the monthly expenses which you have provided, and your employer knows that you cannot pay your monthly bills each month. This type of evidence will make a judge or jury look unfavorably on your employer if your claim ends up in court.

Is Maintenance The Same As Workers' Compensation?

Workers often ask if maintenance is the same as workers' compensation benefits. Workers' compensation benefits are paid under state law when an injury occurs to a worker on land within that state. In contrast, maintenance benefits are paid only to injured seamen under general maritime law. Workers' compensation benefits typically amount to two thirds of the injured worker's average weekly wage at the time of his injury. Unfortunately, maintenance benefits typically amount to $15.00 to $40.00 a day, depending upon the employer of the injured seaman. Note that legally the employer should pay the amount of money it takes for the injured seaman to pay his monthly bills on land. However, it has been our experience that all employers pay a greatly reduced maintenance rate of approximately $15.00 to $40.00 per day despite the actual monthly bills of the injured seaman.

While many individuals are upset when their employers pay such a low amount of maintenance for them to live on each month, we advise our clients that generally their ultimate recovery under maritime law and the Jones Act will be much higher than under a workers compensation law. Pain and suffering damages are not allowed under workers compensation laws, and usually workers compensation benefits are much less than the actual wage loss suffered by the injured worker, especially if the worker cannot return to work after his injury. In such cases, the worker may be able to collect full loss of wages under the Jones Act if his employer was at fault in causing his injury or accident.

Educate yourself today about your rights and options under Maintenance and Cure law, maritime law, and the Jones Act. If you have any questions about your rights, or concerns about your future, call us now toll free at (866) 938-6113 to discuss your situation.

How Can I Get My Monthly Maintenance Amount Increased?

There are at least two ways that we suggest you can try to get your monthly maintenance increased. First, be sure to send your company a written, detailed listing of each of your monthly expenses. Sometimes, but not often, your company may actually increase the amount maintenance based upon legitimate, proven monthly bills that you provide to them.

However, a much better way to increase your monthly maintenance amount is to be sure to file for short-term and long-term disability if you have such policies available to you from your employer. Ironically, most companies discourage injured seamen from applying for short-term and long-term disability. They do this because, in our opinion, most employers want to control the injured seaman's source of income each month. This goes with the overall effort by most employers to control all aspects of your maritime injury claim.

We strongly recommend that anyone with short-term and long-term disability immediately apply for such benefits following a maritime injury. Although many short-term disability policies do not cover work-related injuries, almost all long-term disabilities do cover such injuries. It may take several months for your long-term disability to begin making payments, but at least you will have a source of income much higher than your monthly maintenance payments. This allows you to properly pursue all options and choices that you have against your employer without concern that your employer will terminate your monthly source of income.

ABOUT THE AUTHOR

TIMOTHY YOUNG of The Young Firm practices maritime and Jones Act Law in New Orleans. His office focuses its practice on maritime law claims, representing only injured workers and never maritime or insurance companies. More than 80 percent of his practice involves Jones Act and maritime claims, and his office has successfully represented offshore workers for more than 40 years.

The Young firm is a litigation firm that fully prepares each case that is accepted. Jones Act and maritime claims are strenuously defended by the offshore companies, and to be successful, an injured worker must be prepared to present his case in court.

Mr. Young graduated from Tulane University School of Law in 1993, with Cum Laude honors. He is a member of The American Association for Justice and The Louisiana Association for Justice.

www.ingramcontent.com/pod-product-compliance
Lightning Source LLC
Chambersburg PA
CBHW070932220526
45468CB00005B/1749